COLTER'S RUN

To the Koch Family:
    Hope all your adventures are exciting — and not as dangerous as Colter's Run!

        all best,
        Judith Edwards
        7/19/2001

COLTER'S RUN

Text by Judith Edwards
Illustrations by John Potter

FALCON PRESS

Helena, Montana

Copyright © 1993 by Falcon Press Publishing Co., Inc.,
Billings and Helena, Montana.

Illustrations copyright © 1993 by John Potter.

The author would like to thank Bob Saindon for his ongoing help and
Ruth C. Frick and Shirley H. Winkelhoch, descendents of John Colter,
for new information about Colter's later years in Missouri.

Design, editing, typesetting, and other prepress work by Falcon Press,
Helena, Montana. Printed in Singapore.

Library of Congress Number 92-055080
ISBN 1-56044-178-X

Contents

"Save Yourself If You Can!"

The dry, cactus-covered plain stretched for miles before him. John Colter looked longingly at his moccasins. They lay with the rest of his clothing some 300 yards behind him.

Also behind him were between 500 and 600 Blackfeet Indian warriors, and they wore their moccasins. They also carried bows and arrows and tomahawks. And they didn't look friendly.

"Can you run fast?" asked the old Indian chief who stood beside him.

Colter had a reputation among his fellow hunters and trappers as one of the swiftest runners in the West. But he had a feeling he should keep this information to himself for now.

"No, I've never been a very good runner. And now my ankle is lame from a wound I got in battle," he said.

The chief looked down at the jagged scar on the muscular legs of the young mountain man. He knew about Colter's last Indian battle because he had been there. In the summer of 1808—only three months ago—about 1,500 Blackfeet warriors had attacked a camp of Crow and Flathead Indians. Colter was camped with the Crow, and he had to fight alongside them to save his life.

The Blackfeet were furious that a white man would fight on the side of their traditional enemy. Yet they had a grudging admiration for him, too. On many occasions, Colter had stood up for himself against terrible odds. And he hadn't tried to run away today. He deserved a chance to run for his life—especially since he was probably too lame to outrun them!

The chief untied the thongs that bound Colter's hands behind his back.

"Save yourself if you can," he said.

Colter began to run, trying to ignore the cactus thorns that bit into his feet. The sound of hundreds of fierce war whoops urged him on. He ran faster than he had ever thought possible—not as if his life depended on it, but because it really did!

Ambush in Blackfeet Country

Colter knew that the Madison River lay six miles away across that thorny plain. If he could reach it, maybe he could find a way to escape.

The midday sun beat upon his naked shoulders. His ears rang with the Indians' bloodcurdling cries for vengeance. But the worst of it was that he couldn't avoid the razor-sharp thorns of the cactus that covered the hot, hard plain under his feet. Pain shot up through his whole body. He had no choice but to endure it. He hoped he wouldn't be cut so badly that he wound up running on nothing but bone!

If only he had obeyed his instincts this morning. If only he had turned back instead of listening to his fellow trapper, John Potts. Poor Potts! He was now so full of arrows he looked like a porcupine!

Colter put on a burst of speed at the thought. This morning was only a few hours ago, but it seemed like a century since he and Potts had been picking up their traps in a small stream in what would someday be Montana.

To avoid the hostile Blackfeet, the two mountain men had trapped at night in this early fall of 1808. They worked as quietly as possible and then picked up their traps just at daybreak. This particular morning, as the trappers paddled their canoes down the stream, Colter heard a sound he was sure was the hoofbeat of many horses.

"Listen to that," he said to Potts, who was in a canoe behind him. "There's only one thing that sound can mean—Blackfeet warriors looking for trouble."

He started to turn his canoe around.

"Oh, come on Colter," Potts said with a snicker. "What kind of an old lady are you getting to be? Why, that's nothing but a herd of buffalo a long ways from here. We can get our traps and be out of here extra quick if you're so skittery."

Potts paddled his canoe toward the edge of the stream. The banks were too high for the men to see over them. The sound of pounding hooves grew closer, but instead of turning his canoe and paddling downstream to safety, Colter pulled alongside Potts to argue with him.

"Look, Potts, I don't think it's worth...."

Suddenly, about 500 or 600 Blackfeet warriors appeared on both banks of the stream. They aimed their arrows straight at the trappers' canoes and ordered the men to come ashore. Colter understood the Blackfeet language, and he could see that he and Potts were completely surrounded. So the two men paddled their canoes to an open spot along the bank.

"I Might As Well Prepare to Die"

The moment the canoes touched shore, an Indian yanked Potts' rifle away from him. Colter firmly took it back and returned it to Potts.

"This does not belong to you," he said to the Indian in a calm voice and in the Blackfeet language.

But then Potts made a fatal mistake. He pushed off into the middle of the stream and raised his rifle. Immediately, an Indian shot an arrow into his hip.

"Colter, I am wounded!" Potts cried.

"Come back to shore!" Colter called. "Can't you see we'll never escape?"

But Potts didn't listen. He pointed his rifle at an Indian and shot him dead. The Indians shot back, and poor Potts was pierced with dozens of arrows.

"My poor and foolish friend has been made a riddle of," Colter thought, "and now I have no chance with these Indians. I might as well prepare to die."

But the Blackfeet didn't shoot Colter. Instead, they began to discuss what to do with him. It was one thing to shoot an

unknown trapper who had killed one of their people while trying to escape. But they knew that this man standing so straight and quiet before them was John Colter—explorer, mountain man, and brave white warrior.

The Blackfeet hated Colter, but they also respected him. They decided to kill him slowly to see just how brave and strong he was. They would have some fun with this enemy before they let him escape into death. Maybe they would use him as a human target for their arrows. Or maybe they would tear off each of his limbs one by one and make him watch their dogs gnaw at his bones.

Colter knew about the imaginative but cruel forms of torture the Blackfeet used. He must have been terrified to hear the Indians debate which one to use on him. But he stood silent,

showing no fear. What would be, would be. He would endure it as best he could.

As a child growing up on a frontier farm, Colter had learned to watch and listen. He was born in Virginia in 1774, but he soon moved with his family to what was then the nation's western frontier, the territory of Kentucky. There, Colter spent many hours alone in the woods, looking for tracks that were barely visible, waiting silently to kill just the right deer. And he had brought those expert hunting and woodsman skills to the expedition that had brought him West with Meriwether Lewis and William Clark just four years ago.

Now, surrounded by hundreds of Indian braves thirsty for his blood, Colter faced the biggest challenge of his life. What were his chances of being alive by sundown?

13

A Cold and Dangerous Hideout

Two Indian warriors stripped Colter of his clothes and moccasins. The chief led him away from the river and onto the hard and prickly plain—the plain over which he was now speeding faster than he ever thought he could run.

"I must have covered about half the distance to the river," he thought. "I'll chance losing a little speed and take a look behind me."

What Colter saw over his shoulder terrified him. Most of the Indians were scattered across the plain quite a distance behind him. But one Indian was not more than 100 yards away! And he hoisted a spear over his head, ready to thrust it into Colter's back! Colter ran so fast that blood gushed from his nose from the pressure of his pounding heart.

He was now only a mile from the Madison. He could faintly see the trees that lined the river. But the Indian had gained so much ground that Colter could hear his footsteps. He could almost feel the spear between his shoulders. When he turned to look again, he saw the warrior just twenty yards away. He knew he couldn't outrun the Indian. There must be something else he could do!

Suddenly Colter stopped, whirled around, and spread his arms wide. The Indian was so surprised that he lost his balance and fell..His spear broke in two, and the point stuck in the ground. Colter jerked it free and drove it through the Indian's back, pinning him to the ground. He knew he had no time to retrieve the spear for a weapon, so he ran on.

Soon, the other Indians reached their fallen companion. They began to howl wildly, their way of grieving for the dead. Colter, nearly fainting from exhaustion and covered with blood from his nose, sprinted the last distance to the river.

From the bank, he saw a small island just downstream. Driftwood had piled against it, forming a logjam. Colter swam to the logjam and dove under. Could he get his head above water

between the wedged logs before he drowned? And if he did, would there be enough wood to hide him?

Just as his head popped above the water between two logs, he heard the Indians reach the riverbank. Through gaps in the logs, he could see them wade into the water and climb onto the logjam above him. So far, he was well hidden. But how long would that last?

For the rest of the day, Colter watched the Indians climbing around on the logs above his head. When he had dived in, the water had been warmed by the afternoon sun. But soon night would fall, and with it the temperature. The river would grow colder, chilling him to the bone. But that wasn't the worst of his worries. Colter was most afraid that the Indians would set fire to the logjam!

His arms ached from holding onto the logs. His body ached from the effort of keeping his muscles and breathing still. Finally, after what seemed an eternity, the Indians disappeared into the distance and were heard no more.

Still, Colter waited until there wasn't even a scrap of daylight before he dared to come out. When it was completely dark, he dove from under the logjam and swam as far and as silently as he could down the river. Quietly, stealthily, he emerged from the water and headed into the night.

Seven Days to Fort Lisa

John Colter had done the impossible. He had survived the run for his life! But that was just the beginning of this awful adventure. Now he must try to find his way back to Fort Lisa, his trapping headquarters —a seven-day trip over treacherous rivers and mountains. And he must travel without shoes or clothing in weather that grew colder every day.

His feet were full of cactus thorns. If only he'd had time to take the moccasins from the Indian he killed. And he could certainly use that spear now. He could see wild game all around him, but he had no way to kill animals for food or clothing.

A lesser man might have given up—but not Colter. There was a reason Lewis and Clark had chosen him to be part of their historic expedition in 1804. They would travel 4,000 miles through the Louisiana Territory, to the Pacific Ocean and back. Just as President Thomas Jefferson wanted the best men to lead the expedition, so Lewis and Clark wanted fearless, competent men to go with them. They wanted men who would be eager to explore this western land full of natural wonders. And they wanted men who could help them learn about the many Indian tribes they would meet.

Colter quickly established himself as one of the most valuable members of the expedition. His keen powers of observation and his skill as a hunter were constantly in demand. Once, when the party had split up to search for a river that would take them to the ocean, Clark sent Colter back to Lewis with a letter describing his findings. Clark knew he could count on Colter to deliver the important message. He wouldn't get lost, he would notice things along the way, and if he encountered danger, he would act quickly and calmly—just as he would later do with the Blackfeet.

So when the expedition reached the villages of the Mandan Indians in what is now North Dakota—after more than two grueling years of exploration—the captains were pleased with the services of young Colter. And they were happy to grant his request to turn around and go right back up the Missouri.

At the Mandan villages, Colter met two trappers from Illinois who wanted to trap in the Yellowstone River country that Lewis and Clark had just explored. The two men, John Dickson and Forrest Hancock, invited Colter to go with them.

"If you come with us, we'll share our traps with you," Hancock told him. "Why, with all you know about the country and all we know about trapping, we can make a fortune!"

That was enough to convince Colter, who didn't want to leave the West anyway. He asked the captains if he could leave the expedition at once instead of returning with them to St. Louis.

"Why John," Captain Clark said, "we are pleased to be of service to anyone who has performed his duties as well as you. We'll be glad to allow you the privilege of leaving us now. But we have to ask that nobody else in camp asks for a similar favor."

The other members of the expedition liked Colter, so they agreed to Clark's request. They wished Colter success and waved goodbye as he headed upstream once again.

The survival skills that Colter learned on the expedition served him well on his seven-day journey away from the Blackfeet and back to Fort Lisa. In fact, one of them probably saved his life. While with Lewis and Clark, he learned he could eat the nutritious and even tasty vegetables the early French traders called *pomme blanche,* or white apples. Now, he kept from starving by eating them on the long trip back to the fort.

Colter's Hell

Colter traveled by night through Indian country. He slept huddled under tree branches to keep warm or to protect himself from the blistering sun.

He knew the countryside well. His trapping venture with the two Illinois men had not lasted long. But when it ended, Colter had once again turned around and gone upstream with a group of trappers. The leader of the group was Manuel Lisa, head of the first successful American fur company. He and his men built a fort at the junction of the Bighorn and Yellowstone rivers in the fall of 1807. It was this fort that Colter was slowly and painfully traveling toward now.

Lisa had also recognized Colter's worth as an explorer. When he wanted to encourage the Crow Indians to trade furs at the new fort, he sent Colter to find them. He also instructed Colter to explore the unknown wilderness and learn its topography. Then the traders could make maps of the area. It was these fur traders' maps that helped open the West to settlers later in the century.

No one has ever found a written record by Colter of his
journey to the Crows. He may not have kept a journal. But he did
tell others about the route he took and the wonders he saw.
William Clark made a map of Colter's 1807 travels and named a
river after Colter.

On this important trip, Colter left Fort Lisa and traveled south
along the Bighorn River to the river Clark called the "Stinking
Water" on his map. Today it's known as the Shoshone River.
Then he traveled through the steep, rocky, and often barren
Absaroka Mountains. Did he travel on foot, using snowshoes as
winter came on? Or did he travel on horseback? Did he have
Indian guides, or did he travel alone? How much of his travel was
by land and how much by river? Did he find the Crows'
encampments or meet any Spanish trappers? No one knows the
answers to these questions, but Colter undoubtedly had to rely on
all his considerable skills on this trip.

Colter headed north from what is now Wyoming, crossing the
Teton Mountains. He followed the Teton River and entered what
writers were later to call "Colter's Hell." Here, he saw boiling
sulfur springs and fires that seemed to erupt from the earth.
Today this land of amazing geographical wonders is called
Yellowstone National Park.

Colter was the first white man known to visit Yellowstone. He
must have been amazed to see its bubbling hot springs and
shooting geysers. What did he think of Old Faithful, erupting 170
feet into the air every sixty-five minutes? Or Giant Geyser,
spouting a column of water more than 200 feet into the air for as
long as two hours at a time? When Colter told his fellow trappers
back at the fort about these unbelievable sights, they thought he
was exaggerating.

In 1972, Yellowstone National Park celebrated its 100th
anniversary. Colter's picture decorated a medal commemorating
the event, and on the medal, Colter was credited with discovering
Yellowstone.

Exhausted, Foot-Sore, But Alive!

If the trappers at Fort Lisa had trouble believing Colter when he spoke of the geysers, what would they think when he stumbled naked into the fort with a tale of running for his life from the Blackfeet?

One day, a sentry posted in a tower at Fort Lisa saw a dark object in the distance. It appeared to be headed slowly for the fort.

"Hey," the sentry called to a man below. "Come up here. Either I'm going crazy or there's a man out there."

"Probably an Indian," the other trapper said, climbing quickly into the tower. The two men watched as the scraggly figure came closer. It was a filthy, bearded man, walking as if in great pain. They aimed their rifles in his direction. Then they both cried out.

"That looks like Colter!"

They could barely recognize him. Hungry and weak, he raised his hands over his head and stopped. The gate was thrown open, and his fellow trappers rushed out to welcome him. Because of his own endurance and his remarkable presence of mind, Colter was alive!

After escaping so narrowly with his life, Colter vowed to leave Blackfeet country forever. But there was the matter of those traps he and John Potts had laid. They must still be full of beaver, which meant valuable skins to trade.

"The Blackfeet can't possibly be back in the Three Forks area," he reasoned. "They were moving to their winter encampment when they caught poor Potts and me."

So, in the winter of 1809, he decided to return to the stream where his run for life had started and pick up those traps.

But the Blackfeet *were* there. Just as Colter reached for a trap, their bullets peppered the water in front of him. He left his traps to the fate of the river.

"If I can get out of this country alive, I am surely never coming back!" Colter vowed again as he fled back to Fort Lisa.

Back at the fort, Colter decided to leave the West right away with several men who were taking the year's fur catch to the Mandan villages. There, he would board one of Lisa's supply boats and head down the Missouri River to St. Louis.

Washington Irving wrote about Colter in his book *Astoria, or Anecdotes of an Enterprise Beyond the Rocky Mountains.* In it, Irving compares the western trapper to a sailor who has been on dangerous voyages. No matter how much the "sailor" suffered on his last expedition, he always sails again. And the more adventurous the trip, the more he likes the idea.

So it was with Colter, because he turned around again and headed back up the Missouri to the Yellowstone River area! He rejoined Lisa's company, and in March 1810 he led thirty-two American and Canadian trappers up the Yellowstone to the Three Forks area—Blackfeet country.

Travel was slow because of the heavy snow that year. The sun glancing off the white snow affected the men's vision, and many of them became snowblind. The group saw many signs of the Blackfeet as they entered the area where Colter had begun his grueling run only two years earlier.

Colter decided he had pressed his luck far enough. Although he helped build a trading post at Three Forks in April, he made plans to return to civilization again. Alone, in a small canoe, he traveled the 2,500 miles to St. Louis.

There, in 1810, Colter met a botanist named John Bradbury.

"I saw him on his arrival," Bradbury later wrote, "and received from him an account of his adventures after he had separated from Lewis and Clark's party.''

In his book *Travels in the Interior of America*, Bradbury gives the only firsthand written account of Colter's run. The tale is lively, and he includes many of Colter's own words. No one knows what Colter said or thought as he encountered the Blackfeet and ran across that thorny plain. But Bradbury's detailed account, coupled with a little imagination, helps to bring this exciting historical event to life.

Riding with the Mounted Rangers

After leaving the West in 1810, Colter began to settle down. As part of his pay for the Lewis and Clark expedition, the U.S. government gave him a piece of land. It covered 320 acres in eastern Missouri. Because of problems with the estate of Meriwether Lewis, who had died in 1809, Colter had yet to receive his full pay. He needed cash, so he sold his land.

In May 1811, Colter finally got $375.60 for his part in the Lewis and Clark expedition—a lot of money in those days. Though he had left the expedition in August 1806, he was paid to the last day of October like the rest of the members. This was another measure of how much Lewis and Clark valued Colter's services.

No one knows much about Colter's later life. He married a woman called Sally and settled on land near Dundee, Missouri. He

had one son, Hiram, who eventually had eight children of his own.

When Colter reached St. Louis in 1810, the frontier was no farther west than Missouri. The Indians had been pushed from their land to make room for white settlers, and the tribes were competing with one another for the few remaining hunting grounds. Indians often raided settlement families, and both settlers and Indians lost their lives as treaties were made and broken. The British took advantage of this situation to enlist the Indians against the United States, and this helped to cause the War of 1812. Along the frontier, no one was safe.

Captain Nathan Boone, son of Daniel Boone, was ordered to form a company of mounted rangers to build forts along the frontier. These forts were to protect the white families settled around the Mississippi and Missouri rivers.

Now a small landowner in Missouri, Colter volunteered to serve with the rangers. He had to bring his own food, clothing, rifle, and horse. In February 1812, he borrowed money from William Clark, who was then the Indian agent for the western territories. He used the money to outfit himself for the Mounted Rangers.

The rangers built many forts and acted as troops to protect the countryside. They were described in a letter from Missouri Governor Benjamin Howard to the Secretary of War, William Eustis, as "a fine body of hardy woodsmen as ever took the field." Leader Nathan Boone must have thought highly of Colter's skills. He named a son John Colter Boone.

Colter was supposed to serve with the rangers until June 7, but he was discharged with full pay on May 6. He died a day later, May 7, 1812, probably of jaundice. The years of physical hardship in the West may have finally taken their toll.

Though he was only thirty-eight years old when he died, Colter had packed a great deal of living into those years. Only eight years had passed since he had joined the Lewis and Clark expedition. How many people could boast of a life so full of amazing sights and marvelous adventures? John Colter had even run for his very life—and lived to tell about it!

Highlights from American History Series

Featuring true to life depictions of major historical events, this series introduces young readers to our fascinating heritage and the captivating world of history. Each title is 32 pages, 7x10", $5.95 and includes original color illustrations.

Flight of the Nez Perce. This is the story of the famous retreat and eventual surrender to the U.S. Army which led to Chief Joseph's "I will fight no more forever" speech.

The Lewis & Clark Expedition. Relive the hardships and new discoveries of Lewis & Clark's two-year journey across the Great Plains and the Rocky Mountains to the Pacific Ocean.

The Battle of the Little Bighorn. The story of the famous battle between U.S. Army soldiers and the Sioux and Northern Cheyenne Indians also known as Custer's Last Stand.

Into the Unknown: Major Powell's River Journey. Follow John Wesley Powell's river boat journey to discover what is now known as the Grand Canyon.

Colter's Run. The story of mountain man John Colter's famous escape from Blackfeet warriors and his life of adventure.

Available in local bookstores or from
Falcon Press, P.O. Box 1718, Helena, Montana 59624,
1-800-582-2665

Interpreting the Great Outdoors Series

Nature's wonders—delicate wildflowers, active volcanoes, towering redwoods— are certainly remarkable. Unfortunately, many people—especially young people—know little about them. For this reason, Falcon Press launched this series to help readers ages 8 and older understand the workings of our natural world.

The Fire Mountains. Learn about the once active Cascade volcanoes found in California, Oregon, and Washington.

The Tree Giants. Read about the redwoods, the world's largest trees.

Where Dinosaurs Still Rule. A wonderfully illustrated and informative guide to dinosaur dig sites and museums throughout the West.

Falcon Press publishes and distributes a variety of nature-oriented books and calendars for adults as well as children.

For our free catalog call toll-free 1-800-582-2665 or write to: Falcon Press, P.O. Box 1718, Helena, Montana 59624